Nelson Mandela

by Jill C. Wheeler

921
MANDELA, N

visit us at
www.abdopub.com

Published by ABDO & Daughters, an imprint of ABDO
Publishing Company, 4940 Viking Drive, Suite 622, Edina,
Minnesota 55435. Copyright ©2002 by Abdo Consulting
Group, Inc. International copyrights reserved in all countries.
No part of this book may be reproduced in any form without
written permission from the publisher.

Printed in the United States.

Edited by Paul Joseph
Graphic Design: John Hamilton
Cover Design: Mighty Media
Interior Photos: Corbis and AP/Photo

Library of Congress Cataloging-in-Publication Data

Wheeler, Jill C., 1964-
  Nelson Mandela / Jill C. Wheeler
      p.   cm. — (Breaking barriers)
  Includes index.
  Summary: A biography of the South African leader who became a
civil rights activist, political prisoner, and president of South Africa.
  ISBN 1-57765-639-3
  1. Mandela, Nelson, 1918—Juvenile literature. 2. Presidents—
South Africa—Biography—Juvenile literature. 3. Anti-apartheid
movements—South Africa—Juvenile literature. 4. South Africa—
Politics and government—1994—Juvenile literature. [1. Mandela,
Nelson, 1918- 2. Presidents—South Africa. 3. Civil rights workers.
4. Nobel Prizes—Biography. 5. Blacks—South Africa—Biography.]
I. Title.
  DT1974. W48 2002
  968.06'5'092—dc21
  [B]
                                            2001027935

Contents

World Peacemaker

*B*urundi is among the world's poorest nations. For seven years, a bloody civil war has ravaged this tiny central African country. The fighting has killed more than 200,000 people. More than one million more have been driven from their homes. The fighting has pitted rebel Hutus (HOO-toos) against the Tutsis (TOO-sees). While there are more Hutu people in Burundi than Tutsi people, the Tutsis control the army and the government.

In November 2000, a round of peace talks opened in neighboring Tanzania. The talks sought to bring Tutsi and Hutu representatives together to discuss ending the conflict.

The leader of the peace talks was neither Hutu nor Tutsi. He spoke quietly and calmly. He asked the Hutu rebels to agree to a cease-fire. He urged both sides to cooperate with a new government that represented both sides. He even offered to get them economic assistance to repair their war-torn country.

Nelson Mandela

Nelson Mandela, left, is welcomed by Tanzanian President Benjamin Mkapa at Arusha International Airport, Tanzania, March 26, 2000.

This negotiator for peace was a black African man named Nelson Mandela. Nelson was no stranger to conflict. He had fought a 46-year battle against discrimination in his own native South Africa. Despite nearly 30 years in prison, he never let his anger get the best of him. He knew peace does not always come quickly. He also knew that however long it took, peace—and freedom—were worth the trouble.

"Freedom is indivisible," he once said. "The chains on any one of my people were the chains on all of them, the chains on all of my people were the chains on me."

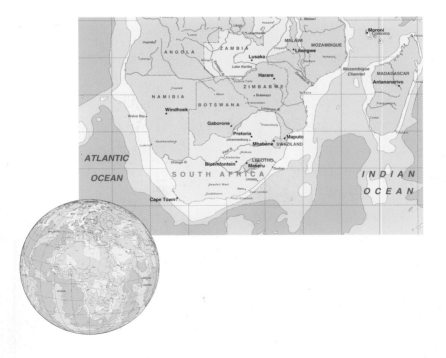

A Boy Named Trouble

*T*he man the world came to know as Nelson Mandela was born on July 18, 1918, in the small village of Mvezo (m-VAY-zoh), South Africa. Mvezo is located on the banks of the Mbashe (m-BAH-shay) River. Nelson's father, Henry Mphakanyiswa (m-pah-kah-NEE-swah) Mandela, named his child Rolihlahla (RHOH-lee-hlah-hlah). Rolihlahla is a Xhosa (KHOH-zah) word meaning "pulling the branch of a tree," or "troublemaker." As a boy, Nelson was called Buti (BOO-tee). He began being called Nelson when he started school.

Nelson's father, Henry, was chief of the small village of Mvezo. His mother, known as Fanny, was Henry's third wife. It was customary at that time in Africa for a man to have more than one wife. Each of Henry's wives had her own household and small farm, or kraal (KRAWL). Henry traveled between those kraals. Nelson had three sisters, three half-brothers, and six half-sisters.

Mud brick huts with straw roofs on a small farm, or kraal, in South Africa.

Nelson's father was a member of the Thembu (TEM-boo) tribe. The Thembu people were part of the Xhosa nation. They had lived, farmed, and raised animals in the region for generations. It was a beautiful land of fertile valleys and rolling hills, with mountains to the west and the Atlantic Ocean to the east. The Thembu people were loyal to a king. Henry served as an advisor to the king.

One day when Nelson was still a baby, there was a problem in his village. A family's ox had wandered off into a neighboring kraal. The people at that kraal did not know the ox belonged to someone else, so they butchered it and ate it. When Henry learned what had happened, he ordered the people who killed the ox to pay the owner for it. They complained to the local English magistrate.

In those days, Great Britain ruled South Africa. The British had their own system of government separate from the tribal government system. The British system governed with a local magistrate. The magistrate who worked in Nelson's region ordered Henry to come see him, but Henry refused. As a Thembu chief, he believed he only had to answer to the Thembu king.

The Thembu government was separate from the British one. However, the British still had authority over Thembu chieftains. Henry didn't see things that way. He believed the British should not have any power greater than that of the Thembu leaders. Henry lost his chieftainship and his possessions because he refused to appear before the magistrate.

Henry knew he had done the right thing. He felt it was important to stand up for his beliefs. He passed that value on to his children. Nelson would live by that value all his life.

Nelson and his mother and sisters moved a few miles away to another village called Qunu (KOO-noo). Qunu had several hundred people living in mud huts with grass roofs. Life in Qunu was much like it had been in Mvezo. Nelson helped herd cattle and played with the other boys using homemade toys. His mother and sisters grew fields of corn, pumpkins, and beans.

Henry was no longer a chief, yet people still looked to him for guidance and help in resolving disagreements. Henry also was a captivating storyteller. He could neither read nor write, so he used stories to pass on the history of the Thembu tribe and Xhosa nation to his family. Likewise, Fanny entertained her children with the same Xhosa fables and legends she had loved as a child.

A reproduction of a South African Kraal.

Adopted by Royalty

*W*hen Nelson was still a boy, he got to know two men who were friends of his father. The men were from a different tribe and had gone to school. As they got to know Nelson, they realized he was very intelligent. They told Fanny she should send her son to school. Fanny had never been to school. Neither had Henry. Yet when she told Henry, he agreed it would be a good idea.

Nelson was seven years old when he started classes at the local missionary school. His father said he needed different clothes for school. Nelson always wore a blanket draped around his shoulder and pinned at the waist. He had no other clothes. His father took a pair of his pants and cut them off at the knee. Then he put them on Nelson and cinched the waist with string. Nelson was very proud of his new pants.

On the first day of school, the teacher gave all the African children English names. That was when Buti first was called Nelson. He wondered if the English

Sitting at their desks, children follow along in their books during a lesson at a school in South Africa.

people gave Africans new names because they thought it was too hard to pronounce their African names.

Nelson's life changed dramatically when he was nine. His father was visiting his mother one evening when he began coughing uncontrollably. He became very ill and died a little later. Fanny told her son he had to leave Qunu. She and Nelson left Qunu and walked a full day to the village of Mqhekezweni (m-kay-KAH-zwee-nee). There Nelson saw wonderful houses and motor cars. It was the home of Chief Jongintaba Dalindyebo (jong-een-TAH-bah dahl-ind-JAY-boh). Dalindyebo was the acting regent of the Thembu people. People called his village the Great Place.

Nelson learned his father had helped Dalindyebo become regent. Because of this, Dalindyebo had offered to become Nelson's guardian when Henry died.

Fanny was sad to leave her son with someone else. However, she knew Nelson would have more opportunities living with the regent. She was right. Dalindyebo and his wife, No-England, treated Nelson the same as they treated their son, Justice. The boys attended a one-room school next to the palace. There they learned English, Xhosa, history, and geography. The village was a mission station of the Methodist Church, so there was more Western influence there than in Qunu. Nelson began to dress in the Western style. He attended the village Methodist Church with Dalindyebo and his family.

Nelson carefully observed activities around the palace. At the tribal meetings, every man there had a chance to speak. Dalindyebo would open the meeting, and then sit silently, listening. He wouldn't speak again until everyone who wanted to had voiced their opinion. Nelson noticed some speakers were more effective than others. He learned what worked and what didn't. He appreciated that the regent worked with the men until they could agree, or agree to disagree. Women were not allowed to participate at that time. Nelson did not see this as unusual as it had always been that way.

Nelson also loved listening to stories of African history. The elders and advisors who came to the palace would tell tales of ancient kings and warriors and their battles. They told stories of people from outside the Xhosa nation, too. This gave Nelson a sense for the full richness of African history.

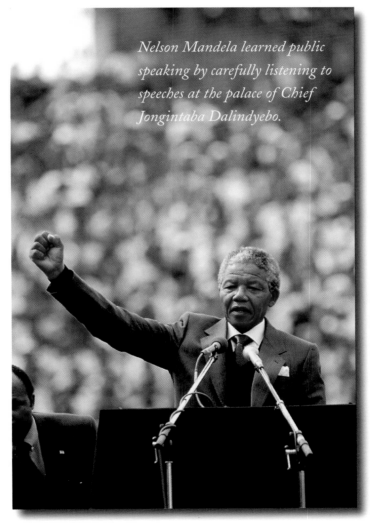

Nelson Mandela learned public speaking by carefully listening to speeches at the palace of Chief Jongintaba Dalindyebo.

Boy to Man

*W*hen Nelson was 16, it was time for him and Justice to participate in a special tribal custom. It was a ceremony where boys became men. Boys had to go through the ceremony if they wanted to marry or gain their inheritance.

Nelson and Justice journeyed to a special place on the banks of the Mbashe River. There, a group of elders took them through the ceremonies. The boys rubbed their bodies with white clay from the riverbank. They dressed in traditional grass skirts. They sang and performed ceremonial dances. Finally, they went through the rites of manhood.

The people of the Great Place held a celebration for the young men when they returned. Nelson was given two cattle and four sheep. He had never felt so rich. Now he was a man in the eyes of the village.

Soon after the ceremony, he left the Great Place for a new adventure. Like his father, he was going to be a counselor to kings. He needed more schooling to do that. He enrolled at Clarkebury Boarding Institute, a high school started by the Methodist Church. Dalindyebo drove him there in his car. It was the first time Nelson had ever been across the Mbashe River.

Nelson Mandela

Nelson graduated from Clarkebury and enrolled at Healdtown. It was a Methodist college, and Justice already was there. At Clarkebury, Nelson had been one of many Thembus. At Healdtown, he was one of many Africans. He met people from other tribes.

English people ran Healdtown. They wanted the African students to learn the same way they had. They also wanted them to act English. They truly believed the English way of living was better than the African way.

Nelson spent two years at Healdtown. Then he and Justice moved to Fort Hare, another missionary college for Africans from all tribes. Nelson studied

Students at a university campus in South Africa.

English, law, and politics. He competed in soccer and cross-country running and joined the drama society.

During his final year, Nelson was nominated to serve on the school's Student Representative Council, or SRC. It was the school's most important student organization. Nelson was honored to be nominated. Before the elections, the students gathered to talk about changes they would like to see at the school. One of their complaints was that the school's food was bad. The students urged the SRC candidates to do something about it.

Nelson agreed the food needed to be improved. In protest, he resigned from the SRC elections. The school's principal told him he must rejoin the council or be expelled. Nelson decided to stand up for his beliefs. He was expelled.

Dalindyebo was angry when Nelson told him what had happened. He ordered Nelson to go back to the school and rejoin the SRC. Then he told Nelson he had picked out brides for him and Justice. It was customary then for families to arrange marriages. However, neither Nelson nor Justice liked the women Dalindyebo had chosen for them. They decided to run away.

They waited until Dalindyebo was gone on a business trip. They sold two of his oxen to get money. Then they packed their suitcases and caught a ride to Johannesburg.

City of Gold

*J*ohannesburg was the largest city in South
Africa. It began as a gold-mining boomtown in the
late 1800s. People from around the world had
traveled there to make their fortune. Africans knew
Johannesburg as the "city of gold." When Nelson
arrived in 1941, the city was busier than ever. It was
the middle of World War II. South Africa was a
member of the British Commonwealth. The South
African people wanted to help the commonwealth
fight Nazi Germany.

Nelson was one of thousands of young Africans
who had come to Johannesburg to work. Many found
jobs in the gold mines. They worked long hours for
low wages. Many got sick from the mine dust.
Meanwhile, the white mine owners became
very wealthy.

Life in Johannesburg was hard for most black
Africans. Nelson was shocked at how much prejudice
he found. Black Africans could ride only certain
buses. They could not eat in most restaurants. They
paid a tax just because they were black. They could
live only in certain parts of the city. These slum areas

on the city's outskirts were called townships. They had no electricity or sanitary sewer systems. Homes were tin-roofed, dirt-floor shacks crowded together. Nelson had to live there as well. There was no other choice.

Young children play in the streets of Sofiatown, a slum section of Johannesburg, South Africa, in 1955.

Dalindyebo soon learned that Nelson and Justice had gone to Johannesburg. He ordered them to return. Nelson asked if he could stay in Johannesburg and continue his education. The regent agreed reluctantly.

Nelson had no job and no money. He found help through a friend named Walter Sisulu. Walter was a real estate agent. He knew a white lawyer who agreed to give Nelson a job as a clerk. Nelson worked for the law firm while he finished his college degree through a correspondence course. He returned to Fort Hare in 1943 for the graduation ceremony. Fanny and No-England also came to the ceremony. Sadly, Dalindyebo had died shortly before Nelson earned his degree.

Nelson returned to Johannesburg and took law classes at night at the University of the Witwatersrand. It was hard for him to get home from his classes before the government-ordered curfew for blacks.

It also was hard to live on the tiny salary he earned at the law firm. Some days he walked the six miles (9.7 km) to work and back to save bus fare. At night, he studied by candlelight because it was cheaper than a kerosene lamp. His boss at the law firm give gave him a suit. Nelson wore it for five years.

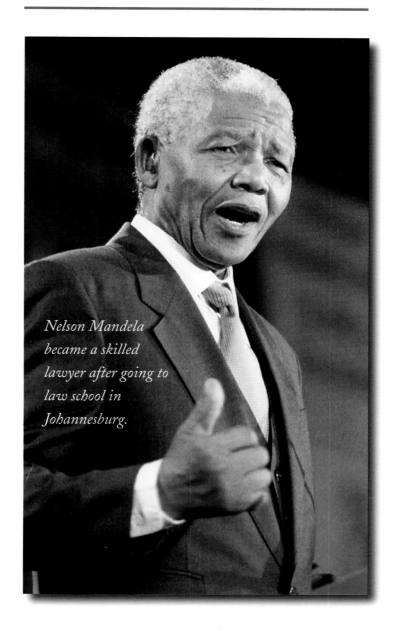

Nelson Mandela became a skilled lawyer after going to law school in Johannesburg.

A man is searched by South African police in an attempt to stop street violence.

In those days, black men had to carry a government-issued pass at all times. Police had the right to stop Nelson or any other black man at any time to see his pass. Blacks who got jobs in white areas of the city had to get special stamps from their employers to put on their passes. They could only enter the white areas with those stamps. Fortunately, the people at Nelson's firm believed the color of a person's skin was not as important.

Nelson met many interesting people at the law firm and the university. He loved to go to Walter Sisulu's house in the evenings and hear black Africans talk about the needed changes in their homeland. Some of those people were members of the African National Congress, or ANC. The ANC opposed apartheid. Apartheid is an Afrikaner word meaning apartness. It also is the name for the South African system of keeping blacks and whites separate and unequal.

Nelson met another special person at Walter's home as well. She was a relative of Walter's, and her name was Evelyn Mase. She was a nurse at a hospital in Johannesburg. Nelson and Evelyn hit it off from the start. They were married several months later.

Birth of an Activist

*I*t wasn't long before Nelson and his friends decided they needed to do more to end apartheid. On Easter Sunday, 1944, they organized the Youth League as a part of the ANC. The Youth League would seek to get black Africans to work together for change. Walter Sisulu became treasurer of the Youth League. One of Nelson's friends from Fort Hare was elected secretary. His name was Oliver Tambo.

In 1947, Nelson was elected general secretary of the Youth League. His new job meant many days on the road traveling around Africa. He met other black African leaders. He encouraged them to work together to fight discrimination.

By 1948, the world was beginning to take notice of the situation in South Africa. The United Nations passed a resolution that condemned South Africa's policies of racial discrimination. Even some white South Africans began to feel their government was doing the wrong thing. However, they were in the minority.

Oliver Tambo

A crowd of South African men are held back by razor wire.

Only whites were allowed to vote in South Africa. Most of these people believed whites were better than blacks and people of color. They called themselves and their political party Nationalists. The Nationalist Party was swept into power in the 1948 elections. They controlled the prime ministership and the legislature. They had one goal: maintain white supremacy.

The Nationalist government began enacting new apartheid laws. The Population Registration Act forced everyone to be classified as one of four races: black, white, colored, or Asian. Colored described mixed-race people.

The race classifications limited what people could do. People could not marry outside their race. They could not attend church or go to the theater with people of other races. Blacks and Asians could not vote at all. All non-whites had to carry government passes if they wanted to work in white areas.

The Nationalist government also created black states in rural Africa. They gave each major African ethnic group one state. The government didn't care if the state was located where the ethnic group lived or not. Many rural Africans had to move from their homes. And while black Africans made up most of the population of South Africa, the black states accounted for only 13 percent of the country's land. It was the most barren and unproductive land, too.

When Nelson earned his law degree in 1953, he and Oliver Tambo set up a law firm in Johannesburg. It was the city's first black law firm. Nelson and Oliver served primarily black clients. The stories their clients told were heartbreaking and unfair. Nelson became even more convinced he had to help end discrimination against black Africans and other people of color.

By this time, Nelson had learned of a new method of fighting injustice. An Indian man named Mahatma Gandhi had started it. People called it passive resistance. Passive resistance allows people to challenge a government by non-violent methods. These methods include refusing to obey orders or laws.

In 1952, the ANC organized an act of passive resistance called the Defiance of Unjust Laws Campaign. On June 26, blacks and people of color around Johannesburg began deliberately breaking apartheid laws. Nelson worked with a group of 50 black Africans to step out into the street after the 11 p.m. curfew. They were arrested and taken to jail. The campaign spread to other parts of the country. Early in July, police began arresting ANC leaders to try to stop the campaign. They raided Nelson's home in the early morning hours. It was the first of many raids on the Mandela home.

Nelson Mandela poses in the law office he opened with fellow anti–apartheid activist Oliver Tambo in Johannesburg, South Africa, in 1953.

At the end of the campaign, more than 8,500 people had broken apartheid laws on purpose. The government responded by banning 52 anti-apartheid activists, including Nelson. When the government banned a person, they were not allowed to join in any group of more than three people. They could not be quoted in the newspaper or on television. They could not have anything published. Banning was how the South African government tried to stop activists from influencing others.

Nelson spent nearly nine years under government bans. As soon as one expired, he would be banned again. "I found myself restricted and isolated from my fellow men," he recalled. "(I was) followed by officers of the Special Branch wherever I went." Despite the ban, he and Oliver continued their law practice. Many of their clients were people arrested because of the Defiance Campaign.

By this time, Nelson and Evelyn had three children and a home of their own. Now it was their turn to help others. Nelson's sister had come to live with them while she attended high school. Fanny also stayed with them and watched the children while Nelson and Evelyn worked. "We made them feel that the house was their own," Evelyn recalled. "Somehow there was always room."

A group of black South Africans burn government passes as violence erupts near Johannesburg.

Congress of the People

*T*hree years after the Defiance Campaign, the ANC and a handful of other groups held a historic meeting. They called it the Congress of the People. Nearly 3,000 delegates attended. The delegates were black, white, Asian, and Colored. They voted to accept a document called the Freedom Charter. The charter began, "We the people of South Africa declare for all our country and the world to know: that South Africa belongs to all who live in it, black and white."

The charter urged a one-person, one-vote policy. It asked that the wealth of South Africa be shared more fairly.

Nelson was proud of the charter. While some black activists wanted a South Africa with no whites at all, Nelson believed differently. He wanted a nation where everyone could live peacefully, regardless of race. The Freedom Charter outlined such a society.

Nelson Mandela

On the second day of the People's Congress, armed military police burst into the meeting hall. They announced no one could leave until their name had been recorded. The police sealed off the building exits. In December 1956, police arrested 156 of the people who had attended the Congress and charged them with treason. Nelson was one of them.

The trial that followed became known as the Treason Trial. It lasted five years. During the trial, Nelson would get up early and take the bus to the courtroom in Pretoria. In the evening, he would return to Johannesburg to work on his law practice and other ANC duties. It was an incredibly stressful time for Nelson and his family. It became so bad that he and Evelyn divorced in 1957.

In the Treason Trial, the government tried to prove that Nelson and the other defendants wanted to overthrow the South African government. They tried to show that the defendants were inspired by communism. They accomplished neither.

In fact, the trial showed that the ANC and the Freedom Charter were multiracial. It helped strengthen support for the ANC and the freedom movement. Demonstrators outside the trial carried signs reading "We Stand By Our Leaders."

In March 1961, the defendants were found not guilty. Among those eagerly awaiting the verdict was a young social worker named Winifred Madikizela (ma-dee-kee-ZAY-la), or Winnie. She and Nelson had been married on June 14, 1958. They had met during the trial and now had two daughters. Winnie breathed a sigh of relief that her husband was free. Sadly, that freedom would be short-lived.

Winnie Mandela

The Black Pimpernel

*N*elson opposed violence. Yet an event in 1960 made him realize the freedom movement might have no other choice. In March 1960, the ANC and another group organized mass protests against the pass law. Protestors marched to police stations and announced they were not carrying their passes. They wanted the police to arrest them.

In the South African township of Sharpville, some 5,000 protestors jammed the streets in support of the campaign. The police feared they were no longer in control of the situation. They called in helicopters. Then they opened fire on the crowd. The protestors turned and ran, but they could not outrun the hail of bullets. When the shooting ended, 69 people were dead, including eight women and children. Many had been shot in the back as they tried to run away. Another 180 people were wounded.

Victims of the 1960 Sharpeville massacre. Sixty nine protesters were killed.

A 1961 photo of Nelson Mandela, then a 42-year-old political activist.

The Sharpville massacre set off another round of protests. The government banned the ANC and the other organization that had organized the pass campaign. Nelson was one of many activist leaders to be jailed. He realized a government willing to shoot unarmed people could not be changed through non-violence. The freedom movement would need to fight fire with fire.

Once Nelson was released from jail, he went into hiding. He was going to organize an armed opposition movement. At the same time, South Africa withdrew from the British Commonwealth. The Nationalist Party chose to withdraw rather than face constant opposition on apartheid from the other Commonwealth nations. The Nationalists planned to celebrate their new independence on May 31, 1961. Nelson and the ANC had other ideas.

For two months, Nelson worked and traveled in secret to organize a May 31 strike for students and workers. He used a false name and disguises to stay one step ahead of police. They had heard about the proposed strike and wanted to stop it. They arrested many activist leaders, but they really wanted to arrest Nelson. They never found him. Journalists began calling Nelson the Black Pimpernel. It was a reference to a literary character called the Scarlet Pimpernel. The Scarlet Pimpernel always avoided capture by his enemies.

The Nationalist's May 31 celebration wasn't much of a celebration. Nearly half the country's students and workers stayed home. Nelson remained in hiding to organize more activities. He had to stay away from Winnie and his children for months at a time because he knew the police would be watching his home.

The armed opposition Nelson had envisioned went into action December 16. Bombs exploded in several South African cities. Nelson's plan was to bomb police, military, and other government buildings to show the ANC was serious about freedom. He advised his colleagues to harm only property—not people. He even went out of the country illegally to drum up support for the cause among other African nations. This trip also helped him learn how to wage a guerilla campaign.

Nelson's fugitive days ended in August 1962. The police finally caught up with the Black Pimpernel. He was arrested and charged with illegally leaving the country and encouraging a strike. In the trial, Nelson served as his own defense lawyer. He admitted encouraging the strike and leaving the country. Then he gave an impassioned speech about why he did it.

Protesters make their way through a burning barricade in a township west of Johannesburg.

"I consider myself neither legally nor morally bound to obey laws made by a parliament in which I have no representation," he said. "In a political trial such as this one, which involves a clash of the aspirations of the African people and those of whites, the country's courts, as presently constituted, cannot be impartial and fair."

The judge sentenced Nelson to five years in prison. He was transferred to Robben Island in May 1963. Robben Island is a desolate, maximum security prison seven miles off the coast of Cape Town.

Several months later, Nelson returned to Pretoria for another trial. This time the state charged him with sabotage and trying to overthrow the government. He knew he could be put to death. This new trial began in October 1963. It lasted five months.

Once again, Nelson used the trial to explain his actions. "I have always regarded myself... as an African patriot," he said. "I have cherished the ideal of a democratic and free society in which all persons live together in harmony with equal opportunities. It is an ideal which I hope to live for and to see realized. But if needs be, it is an ideal for which I am prepared to die."

Nelson and the other defendants were indeed prepared to die. However, the world was watching. Human rights activists from around the world were pressuring the South African government to be merciful. South African authorities knew there would be an international outcry if they executed the defendants.

On June 11, all but one of the defendants was found guilty. They were sentenced to life in prison. Nelson was taken back to Robben Island. He would remain behind bars for the next 27 years.

Nelson Mandela spent 27 years in South African prisons.

Political Prisoner

*N*elson spent the first 18 years in the harsh conditions at Robben Island. His cell was so small he could walk from one end to the other in three steps. He slept on a straw mat on the stone floor. His threadbare blankets offered little warmth. During the day, he and the other prisoners hammered large stones into gravel.

Robben Island was a maximum security prison, the bleakest in the South African system. Nelson was locked up with other political prisoners. The guards did not want the political prisoners around the other prisoners. They were afraid they would spread their ideas of freedom.

As the days went on, Nelson and his fellow prisoners became more depressed. When they left the courtroom, they were pleased to have escaped the death penalty. Some thought the public outcry over their sentencing meant they would be freed soon. As time passed, their dreams of freedom dwindled. "We were face to face with the realization that our life would be unredeemably grim," Nelson remembered.

In 1994, Nelson Mandela revisited the jail cell on Robben Island where he was imprisoned.

"In Pretoria, we felt connected to our supporters and our families. On the island, we felt cut off, and indeed we were."

Life in prison followed a standard routine. Nelson and the other prisoners were awakened each day at 5:30 A.M. Each day they had to clean the bucket they had in each cell in place of a toilet. They had to go through a daily inspection, much like in the military. They were allowed only one letter every six months. Any letters they received were censored, and often had missing parts. The prison allowed few visitors. Sometimes Nelson went years between Winnie's visits.

Even in prison, there was discrimination. Colored and Asian prisoners received slightly better food than blacks. Nelson lived on bad-tasting corn porridge with an occasional old vegetable or gristly piece of meat. He routinely asked for better food, better clothing, and better treatment. He would not accept it if it was just for him. He insisted that all prisoners receive better treatment.

The prisoners only had each other for support. They learned how to steal conversations when the guards were not watching. The prison authorities allowed no music, so he and the other prisoners would sing together when possible. Nelson used his time in prison to help educate other prisoners. He also used his legal skills to represent them in times of trouble. Prisoners often were charged with the most trivial crimes. Nelson once spent three days in solitary confinement with no food because he was caught reading a newspaper.

Nelson and the others learned it was important to behave well toward their guards. Sympathetic guards treated them better and let them talk more. Some guards were even willing to talk with them about their struggle for freedom. Nelson realized the white guards had been told they should fear and hate the black prisoners. They had been told the blacks wanted to kill the whites if they ever achieved power. Nelson told the guards this was not their plan. They wanted a nation where blacks, whites, and people of color lived together in peace.

A young man removes graffiti reading "Free Mandela" from a wall of King's College Chapel in Cambridge, England, in 1965.

At Robben Island, Nelson endured humiliation, discrimination, and malnutrition. Yet he never lost sight of his dream. "I have found that one can bear the unbearable if one can keep one's spirits strong even when one's body is being tested," he said. "Strong convictions are the secret of surviving deprivation; your spirit can be full even when your stomach is empty."

The prison system moved Nelson to Pollsmoor Prison in Cape Town in 1982. There he had a real bed and better food. Nelson believed he and several other prisoners had been moved because they had been successful in generating support on Robben Island for the ANC. At Pollsmoor, he found himself reconnected to the world. He learned the fight for freedom in South Africa had grown increasingly violent. As the ANC stepped up its efforts, the Nationalists responded in kind. The death toll was rising.

In January 1985, South African President P.W. Botha offered Nelson his freedom on one condition. Nelson had to promise to renounce violence. It was the sixth time the government had offered him freedom in exchange for something else. In the 1970s, the government offered him a chance to leave if he promised to recognize the system of black states in rural South Africa and move to his former homeland. He refused.

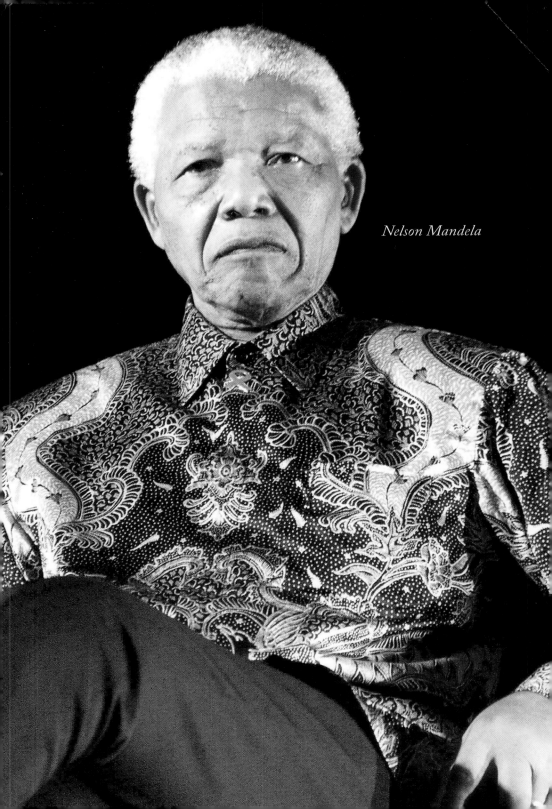

Nelson Mandela

This time, he wrote a speech in response. One of his daughters gave the speech for him. It was the first time people had heard from Nelson in more than 20 years. In the speech, Nelson talked about why the ANC had resorted to violence. He said he could not give up the struggle when so many people had died for it. "Only free men can negotiate," he concluded. "Prisoners cannot enter into contracts."

The authorities moved Nelson again in 1988, this time to a small house within the Victor Verster Prison. Outside the prison, the situation in South Africa grew even worse. International pressure mounted. More countries stopped doing business in South Africa. Sanctions increased. Nelson continued to write letters to the government, requesting talks. President Botha stepped down. F.W. de Klerk took over. Nelson began writing to de Klerk to request a meeting.

President de Klerk proved to be a ray of hope for Nelson and the ANC. In October 1989, he freed eight political prisoners, including Walter Sisulu. He opened South African beaches to people of all colors. The end of segregation of other public places such as parks, theaters, and restaurants was to follow. Nelson had believed de Klerk was loyal to the Nationalist Party. As time went on, he realized de Klerk also understood that things simply had to change.

Nelson met with de Klerk in December 1989. The two discussed many things. Nelson felt the new president truly listened to him. In February 1990, de Klerk began to dismantle the apartheid system. On February 11, he freed Nelson Mandela.

South African President F.W. de Klerk

Free at Last

*N*elson immediately resumed his work to
secure freedom for all South Africans. In June 1990,
he began a world tour to persuade leaders of other
nations to continue their economic sanctions against
South Africa. He also worked with the ANC and
South Africa's ruling Nationalist Party to stop the
ANC's use of violence in their struggle for freedom.

On July 7, 1991, the ANC elected Nelson as their
president. His friend and colleague, Oliver Tambo,
was elected national chairperson. They began
negotiating with the National Party to end apartheid
once and for all. After nearly two years of
negotiations, they reached an agreement. The ANC
and Nationalist Party would partner in ruling the
country for five years, during which time they would
change to a more equal democratic system.

African National Congress deputy president Nelson Mandela, right, shakes hands with Clarence Makwetu, president of the Pan Africanist Congress in Harare, Zimbabwe, April 15, 1991. The two leaders met to bury their differences and find ways to fight a united campaign against apartheid in South Africa.

A New South Africa

Nelson's lifelong dedication to peace and equality was recognized with a Nobel Peace Prize in 1993. South African President F.W. de Klerk received a Nobel Prize at the same time. Nelson accepted his award in the name of all South Africans who suffered and sacrificed to end apartheid. "These countless human beings, both inside and outside our country, had the nobility of spirit to stand in the path of tyranny and injustice, without seeking selfish gain," he said in his acceptance speech. "They recognized that an injury to one is an injury to all and therefore acted together in defense of justice and a common human decency."

Upon his return to South Africa from the Nobel awards in Oslo, Norway, Nelson launched his presidential campaign. In April 1994, the ANC won a majority in South Africa's first-ever all-race elections. In May, the national assembly chose Nelson Mandela as the first-ever black South African president.

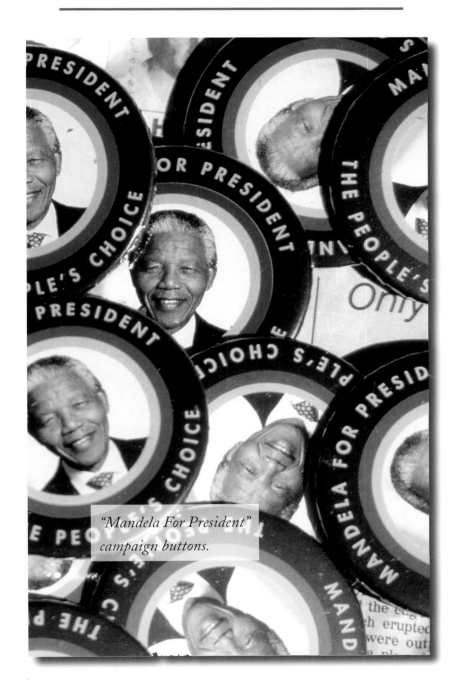

"Mandela For President"
campaign buttons.

"I stand before you filled with deep pride and joy," he said after his election. "Pride in the ordinary, humble people of this country. You have shown such a calm, patient determination to reclaim this country as your own. And joy that we can loudly proclaim from the rooftops: Free at last!"

Nelson refused to use his new position for revenge against the people who had hurt him. In fact, he led an effort to adopt a new South African constitution that banned discrimination against all of the country's minorities—including whites. That constitution was adopted in December 1996. It included sweeping human-rights and anti-discrimination guarantees.

Nelson presided over the government of South Africa until June 1999. During his term, he was divorced from Winnie. Winnie had been suspected in the murder of a young man who had been kidnapped while Nelson was in prison. That complication led to their separation in 1992. He married Graca Machel in 1998 on his 80th birthday.

Nelson has been busy in his retirement. He returned to his old village of Qunu to spend time with his new wife and grandchildren. In 1994, he published his autobiography, *Long Walk to Freedom.*

Nelson stays active helping other nations achieve peaceful resolutions to their conflicts. He also has issued pleas to the world to help Africa battle AIDS. Where there is conflict and discrimination, Nelson is ready to do what he can to help.

"I have discovered... that after climbing a great hill, one only finds that there are many more hills to climb," he wrote in his autobiography. "...with freedom comes responsibilities, and I dare not linger, for my long walk is not yet ended."

Nelson Mandela

Timeline

July 18, 1918: Nelson Mandela born in village of Mvezo, South Africa.

1927: After father's death, goes to live with Jongintaba Dalindyebo, a tribal chief.

1941: Moves to Johannesburg, South Africa.

1943: Organizes Youth League as part of African National Congress (ANC).

1953: Earns law degree, sets up law firm with Oliver Tambo in Johannesburg.

1956: Arrested and charged with treason after helping organize People's Congress.

1960: Sixty nine anti-apartheid protesters killed at Sharpville massacre.

1961: Found not guilty in Treason Trial. Goes into hiding, organizes armed opposition to South African apartheid government.

1962-63: Arrested, convicted of sabotage and trying to overthrow the government.

1990: Released from prison by President F.W. de Klerk, who begins to dismantle the apartheid system.

1991: Elected president of African National Congress.

1993: Wins Nobel Peace Prize.

1994-99: Elected president of South Africa.

Where on the Web?

http://www.anc.org.za/people/mandela.html

A biography of Nelson Mandela from the African National Congress (ANC) web site.

http://www.pbs.org/wgbh/pages/frontline/shows/mandela/

A biography of Nelson Mandela from PBS's Frontline.

http://www.anc.org.za/people/mandela/

The African National Congress (ANC) web site provides text of several of Nelson Mandela's speeches, lists his awards and accomplishments, and provides several photographs.

http://archives.obs-us.com/obs/english/books/Mandela/Mandela.html

Excerpts from Nelson Mandela's autobiography, *Long Walk to Freedom*.

Glossary

African National Congress - ANC
South African political organization that worked to gain civil rights for black Africans.

Afrikaner
A South African descended from Europeans.

apartheid
A policy of racial segregation formerly found in South Africa.

British Commonwealth
An association of nations that accept the British king or queen as their symbolic leader.

Burundi
A nation in east central Africa.

Civil War
A war between opposing groups of people in the same country.

communism

The concept or system of society in which the major resources and means of production are owned by the community instead of individuals.

Hutu

The majority of people who live in Rwanda and Burundi.

kraal

A small farm.

Mahatma Gandhi

An Indian lawyer and political activist who worked to gain India its independence from Great Britain.

regent

A person who rules for the king.

Tutsi

The minority of people who live in Rwanda and Burundi.

Xhosa

A tribal group descended from the Bantu people of Africa. Also the name of the language they speak.

Index